Dedication:

Dedicated to all of the first responders and health care workers. Thank you!

In The Kingdom of Fun, all the children would play.

They would run, jump and climb every single day.

The Castle itself was the most fun place to be,

and the princess and prince hosted the most epic parties.

Swings and slides, games of tag, of course,

and all the children loved taking rides on their amazing pet horse.

Everything was wonderful, until one day,

when something strange happened. The sky even turned grey.

The King was awakened and startled from bed,

as he was told of the arrival of the dreaded Duke of Covid.

The Duke was known as a very dangerous man,

who brought sickness and sadness to all of the lands.

The King was concerned for the safety of all,

and shutdown the Kingdom for all people, both BIG and small.

No schools were open, no parties to be had.

SCHOOL

Closed

The children missed their friends and were all very sad.

Not knowing what to do or where to start,

everyone was told to stay 6 feet apart.

Then out of nowhere who could it be?

Why, it was the bravest of all, The Great Knight Fauci!

The battle ensued. The Great Knight took The Duke to task,

Wielding his sword, while wearing his face mask

As the dust settled it was finally clear.

The Great Knight was victorious, and The Duke of Covid disappeared.

The princess and prince jumped with joy,

and hosted a huge party for all the other
girls and boys

They had games and cake and cheered with glee.

They toasted and thanked The Great Knight Fauci.

As The Great Knight left The Kingdom of Fun,

he said one last thing to everyone:

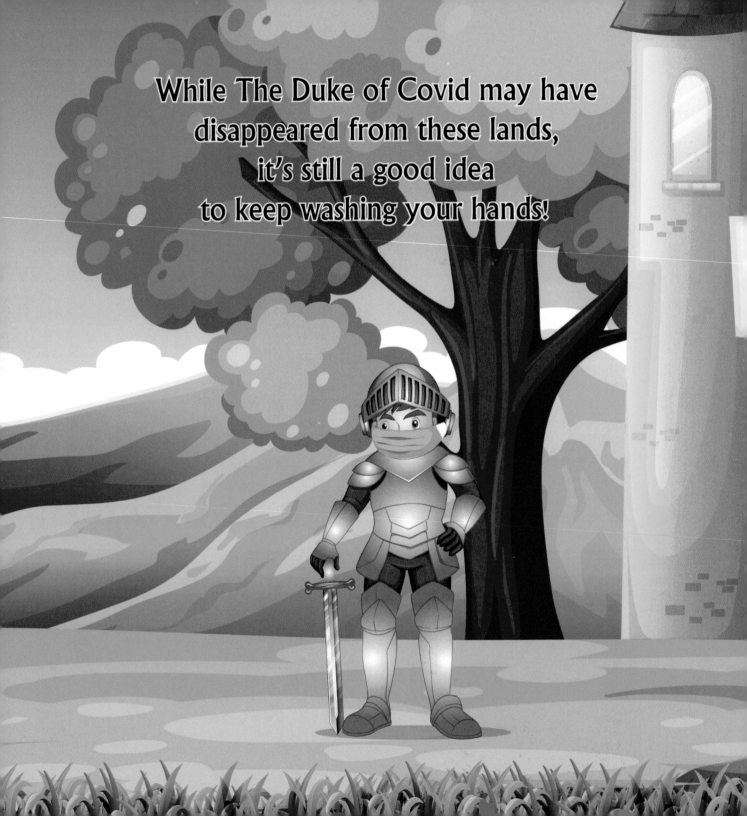

While The Duke of Covid may have disappeared from these lands, it's still a good idea to keep washing your hands!

Made in the USA
Middletown, DE
18 October 2020